A Portsmouth Miscellany
Volume 1

When we print our books within a few weeks we normally hear from people as to why their family business is not mentioned or why did you not include... The answer is because none of our class members or contributors knew of it. We do keep the recollections from people and sometimes at a later date when we update a booklet we can then add the memories in. At other times we are not going to update for some years or produce a booklet on the area they have some memories of, hence this booklet, a Portsmouth Miscellany Volume 1 which records these. We will add pictures when we can to the stories to aid your recollections but obviously the style of the booklet will be different from the 'house style' that we have developed when looking at an area.

The picture on cover shows the High Street in 1956.

GW00584791

Our first set of memories are of growing up in the Kingston Crescent area in the 1940s and come from an overseas contributor now living in New South Wales Australia.

More memories of Kingston Crescent and Area

"I was the youngest in a family of four children, born in 1933 and attended Flying Bull Lane Infants and Boys Schools. We lived at 45 Kingston Crescent before moving across to 98 Kingston Crescent in about 1940 where my family lived for many years.

96-92 Kingston Crescent, now Aldi

We lived next door to Miss Lily Flowers, a spinster, who was a delightful lady. She regularly invited my two sisters, my brother and me to tea. We would, at her request, go to her house [100 Kingston Crescent] in our uniforms. My eldest sister was in the air cadets, my youngest sister a Brownie, my brother a Scout and I, a Naval Cadet. Miss Flowers would have her cook/housekeeper prepare beautiful sandwiches and fairy cakes which we ate with a glass of fresh milk. Generally this was taken in the garden, which was an absolute picture with rolling lawns and flower beds. She always showed a great interest in what we were doing. As a child the mural of trees and country scenes painted around the dining hall, a truly beautiful room, fascinated me. She had a number of brothers who were named after kings and her sisters were named after flowers.

Kingston House (100) and 98 Kingston Crescent (Now Doctors)

In 1949 I moved away. As memories fade I thought no more of it until I was sent a copy of an article published in the Portsmouth Evening News dated January 20, 1965.

"As people wait for the bus in Kingston Crescent, they often stand and stare at Kingston House [100 Kingston Crescent]. Stare and wonder what lies behind those shuttered windows? Who lives there?
And yet the brass door knob shines still, and in one window where the

3

heavy brown Venetian blinds are broken, a square of blue gingham hangs in its place. But it was pink last week, and was there not a lace curtain there the other day?

The last person to live in the house was Miss Lily Flowers who died this month [Jan 1965] aged 90. As a child she lived there with her family, but later lived there alone until five years ago. After a fall downstairs, Miss Flower's doctor recommended that she left the house and she sold to Mrs Ada Langley who lives at 96 Kingston Crescent. She still polishes the door knob and changes the piece of curtain that hangs in the window to repel any positive action from the more inquisitive people who stand and wonder at the bus stop.

Mrs Langley suggested that I may like to look over the house and gave me the keys. As the heavy front door swung open, the silence of the empty house pervaded. It is silent now, but surely the walls once echoed to the voices of children. The crying of babies.

The reception rooms on the ground floor are spacious, but the light which infiltrated through the shutters was subdued, making it difficult to see. The greatest surprise came when I discovered the banqueting chamber. It was the sort of room that one would never expect to find in a private house. It belonged to a different era, and would seem more befitting in a castle, or at least a mansion. Stretching the entire width of the house, and two storeys in height, the room was built for the days when one sat down for meals in style. One could imagine the scene .. the huge trestle table laden with food, the fashionable company, and one could imagine how these walls once rung in laughter and gaiety, the pouring of wine into silver goblets. And now...? Silence. High up on the walls of the chamber there is a painted frieze running right around the room. It is dirty and a lot of it is missing but it still captures the imagination as it has captured the activities of the people it portrays.

The construction of the house is full of oddities that we can now laugh at as eccentricities of the past. For example, the lavatory, which has two doors one of which was lined with felt to muffle the sound. Then there was the shaft down to the cellar where the beer barrels were rolled down, and the old fashioned serving hatch into the corridor leading to the banqueting room.

Kingston House still retains a large amount of land. It is uncommon nowadays in Portsmouth to find a great deal of empty ground behind this

Regent Cinema, 59 London Road (Now Co-op Supermarket)

house the brambles and nettles stretch back as far as the Essoldo Cinema. Mrs Langley said that when Miss Flowers lived there the garden was a joy to look at with roses and other flowers in profusion."

The News 1965

[The house was demolished in Nov 1976 after a partial collapse of the property made it unsafe - Ed]

My paternal grandfather worked for Smith and Vosper's Bakery delivering bread and cakes by horse and cart. The cart was quite high with a van like structure. The padded driver's seat was under an overlap of the roof and had a foot board. One had to use a step to get into the driving seat. On school holidays when I was about eight years old I would accompany my grandfather and feel so proud and important sitting up there with him. As we went along little boys would sometimes swing on the back of the van and grandfather would swish his whip around the back to make them get off.

My maternal grandfather was a passenger guard for Southern Railways and he used to take me down to Portsmouth Town Station and buy me a 'Double Six' block of chocolate. On one occasion he let me print my name on a strip of metal from the machine where one would move a pointer around to a given letter or number, then press down on a handle to stamp it. I attached the completed strip to my school satchel and had it for many years.

When I was about eight years old and each Saturday morning we attended the film club at the Regent Cinema on London Road. We would watch various cowboy films starring either Tom Mix, Hopalong Cassidy, Roy Rogers or Gene Autrey. Also a Flash Gordon serial, each episode finishing with a terrible disaster about to befall him; the next week he would escape unscathed and go from one crisis to another. There would be prizes handed out with an 'Uncle' and 'Aunty' up on the stage with a spotlight shining on them. 'Uncle' had a mirror with which he would reflect the light around the cinema until he picked out someone in the crowd and shone the reflection directly onto their face. 'Aunty' would then come down and give that person a prize. We loved it and looked forward each week to go again.

The Admirals Head public house situated on the corner of Kingston Crescent and Gamble Road. I was probably about nine years old, when I went twice a week to the little 'Bottle Shop' (a small room between the main bar and the lounge) to collect a large bottle of Brickwood's Brown Brew, BBB, for my grandmother

The Admirals Head, Kingston Crescent 1979 (Now Pizzas)

who used to enjoy a glass of beer and a piece of bread and cheese before retiring to bed. The White Hart on Kingston Crescent/Kingston Road corner and opposite the Blue Anchor was a favourite troop's location during the war. On many occasions, a fight would break out between the various nationalities and the American and British Military Police would rush there, the Americans would wade into everyone with their batons in order to bring the situation under control. I asked my father on several occasions, 'If we are all fighting Hitler, why do the troops fight each other?' 'That's the way of the world' was his answer. This meant nothing to me at the time.

Another occasion I recall quite vividly was an episode late one night when there was this terrible noise of galloping horses. My brother and I looked out of the bedroom window and saw a huge pack of carthorses stampeding down Kingston Crescent, I have no idea how many. When they reached the traffic lights at Kingston Cross, the traffic lights were red. Unbelievably the panicking horses stopped and pawing the ground, snorting and whinnying they waited until the lights turned green, then off they galloped along London Road towards North End. That was an incredible sight and one I can never forget. Apparently the horses had come from Bailey & Whites timber yard on Commercial Road which had been bombed and was well alight. The workers had opened the stables and drove out the horses to avoid them being burnt to death.

Another macabre story, which I believe is true, was that a Policeman during an air raid was reporting to the Police Station that was situated at Kingston Cross across the road from Kingston Crescent. A bomb landed and a large piece of shrapnel killed him by blowing off his head. The corpse continued across the road into the station and then fell off the bicycle. He had travelled about 20 yards after being killed. My father occasionally repeated this story, years after the war had ended.

On a less dramatic note there was a small tobacconist shop on the north west corner of Kingston Cross, next to Burton's Mens' Wear, where I would collect my grandfather's tobacco order. It was made up while I waited. The smell of tobacco was wonderful. There was a small gas flame on the counter burning all the time so that customers could light their pipe or cigarette. I liked going there.

Opposite the Lido there were some old disused dams of water. There were items made of wood lying there consisting of two long boxes joined by slats nailed from one to the other. We use to launch these and propel them with a long pole and engage in battles trying to upset the opponents into the water. Looking back it was dangerous but in our ignorance great fun. Another hobby we had was going out after an air raid with a bucket of water and coal tongs collecting shrapnel and bullet casings, plunging them into the bucket to cool them as sometimes they were still hot. We either kept them or exchanged them for other things.

When I was about 11 years old I managed to get a job sweeping up at the Bevis Road Garage and Taxi Company. I was paid three shillings a week. After I had been there for several months I was allowed to fill cars with petrol. This entailed cranking a long handle back and forth until a glass bowl on top of the pump, which held one gallon, was filled up. After placing the nozzle into the car's petrol tank filler, I would turn a handle on the nozzle to allow the petrol, via gravity, to go into the tank. This had to be done for each gallon. There was also a line etched in the sight glass to indicate half a gallon. Cranking the handle was hard work so it was good that there were not many cars. As this job was considered a privilege I was not paid anymore money.

I later left and got a job with Percy Tuck, newsagent at North End. He was a difficult man to work for but paid ten shillings a week delivering papers twice a day. On Saturday evenings, if he liked you, you could earn an extra shilling and sixpence by selling 'The Green Un', a newspaper containing all the football results. Sundays was the day to deliver all the magazines, these were very heavy and the round was much bigger. I got the sack because I asked for an extra sixpence as I was doing a normal daily round and a half but only being paid two shillings.

When I was about 12 years old there was a milkman in Gamble Road (whose name I cannot recall) [Harry Quennell, Kingston Dairy -Ed] who employed me to help him deliver milk. He had a horse drawn yellow two wheeled cart built like a chariot in which there were several churns placed around the sides and across the front with half pint and pint ladles hanging inside them. The ladies of the houses would come out from with their jugs and we would ladle out the amount required. The unattended horse would slowly walk along the road keeping up with us. At the end of the road we would climb aboard and the horse would take us to the next street and we would repeat the exercise until the round was over. The horse knew exactly what was going on; so when we climbed aboard to go back to the stable he would start off at a trot. I would hold the reins and pretend to be driving him, but he knew the way so well that the milkman stood with his back against the side and would complete his book work. On arrival he would unharness the horse as I put food in the trough, and checked the drinking water then let him in the stable and left to go to school. On Sundays I would, under supervision at first, muck out the stable and wash the horse. The horse was a beautiful animal and using a brush and curry comb I would smarten him up making his brown coat shine ready for Monday. I never knew the horse's name as the milkman always referred to him as 'Me old fella'."

Kenneth Frampton, NSW Australia

Our second story concerns Old Portsmouth and should have been in the revised version of 2009 but was omitted in the final edited version supplied to the printers.

Old Portsmouth in the 1950/60s

"The 1960s were a very lively time in Old Portsmouth there were still bomb sites where my children and their friends played imaginative games often involving a home made box-on-wheels, but the rebuilding was going on apace. It was only in 1950 that the decision was made to permit the building of private houses in Old Portsmouth where it had been designated for semi industrial development despite having the cathedral at its centre.

9

When private development was permitted only a few plots were acquired by individuals, the first house to be built was Pharos in Penny Street and then the Doctor's house and surgery on the High Street, both designed by local architect Mike Goodair. After that other sites were acquired by the Cecil Claxon or Mr Sadler [hence the Reldas flats -ed] who built much of the rest. The City planners considered building 'social' housing in Oyster Street decided that their residents would not put up with the noise of shipbuilding behind them and left the site for private development. The only building put up by the City were the flats on the High Street next to the Dolphin.

Buildings on the seaward side of the doctor's surgery were Monck's Oyster Bar which still sold oysters and the original Fountain Inn which featured in a work by George Meredith and housing the YMCA. George Meredith was born in a house on the other side of the road, destroyed in the war, the plaque which marked the house also disappeared. There were two or three elegant regency houses two of which had been banks now converted to private dwellings and the Sallyport run by Mr and Mrs Clapham.

One abiding memory I have is of the then Provost of the Cathedral, the Very Rev Eric Porter-Goff, leading the choir and congregation on Rogation Sunday to 'Beat the Bounds' round the boundaries of Old Portsmouth and pausing at each big site, Power Station, Camber, Barracks to pray.

There was still the coal fired power station depositing black grit on window sills and washing, shipbuilding at Vosper Thorneycroft launching small fast naval craft into the Inner Camber, coal being delivered to Fraser & Whites in the Camber, engineering firms in White Hart Lane and Oyster Street, boat building in Broad Street with George Feltham building wooden 'pulling' boats and sailing dinghies; both he and Harry Feltham building sailing yachts for local people. The floating bridge was taking people and vehicles across to Gosport and the Isle of Wight ferries docking at the East Street slipway.

There were several shops, a busy Post Office and newsagents in Broad Street, Whymark's grocery shop run by Mrs Jones in Oyster Street and three shops on the Lombard Street corner of the Cathedral Green which during the 60s moved over the other side of the High Street, the greengrocer Wain, and butcher known affectionately as Egger though not the barber shop as the barber died. On the corner of Pembroke Road was Vosper the baker, Mr Price the chemists, so two shops on each corner of High Street and Pembroke Road. Further up the High Street was a mattress factory on the corner of Barrack Street which was the name then of Peacock Lane. Further north a garage run by the Bartlett family,

High Street with old shops in front of Cathedral and bomb sites

opposite that were big shed like buildings where the electricity offices were before they built on the corner of Lombard Street and St Thomas's Street [Now a block of flats -Ed]. Behind that in Lombard Street were stables for the horses which pulled Fraser & Whites coal carts and of course at that time Oyster Street continued past St Thomas's Street to join up with White Hart Lane.

Because the power station was still working there was a warm water outfall near the Sallyport, very popular with swimmers and line fishermen too because it attracted numbers of bass which one of my sons liked to catch. There was also frequent flooding of Broad Street which was stoically dealt with by the residents there when high tides at the equinox coincided with a south westerly wind. Most of them had flood boards to insert at the front door packed round with putty and the stone floors on the ground floor and with enough warning they could move vulnerable possessions upstairs. We donned our Wellington boots in order to continue to visit Mrs Mac's restaurant, 'Grogans' a great favourite with the locals and small boat sailors. We even rowed down to it!

The Camber itself still had old wooden sheds at 'Dirty Corner' where my children learned to row and one famous winter so cold that there were ice floes in the Camber and moorings were dragged out into the harbour and the sea by the ice as it broke up and floated away."

Mrs Eddings

Our next memories deal with the difficult times that families went through.

Hard Times But Happy, My Life in Portsmouth

"My Mother and Father were both born and brought up in Sussex. Dad was in the Army and had lost a leg during the Boer War. He had a wooden leg with a leather strap that went over his shoulder. He would hang his leg on the bottom of the bed at night and he never took the shoe and sock off. I remember that the sock was kept up with a drawing pin.

After he was invalided out of the Army, Dad had great difficulty in finding employment in Sussex and only managed to find temporary and short term work. With the end of the First World War it was even more difficult as there were millions of men in the same position, many of them invalids like my Dad. With my five older brothers and sisters to support, things became impossible and even resulted in a short stay in the workhouse. Just before I was born Dad decided to try his luck in Portsmouth and they packed all their belongings onto my sister's pram and walked all the way from Chichester to Portsmouth. This journey took more than a day as they had to sleep rough for at least one night. However, this move proved unsuccessful and Dad never worked again, his health deteriorated even more and he eventually ended up in a wheelchair.

Mum and Dad found accommodation in Flat 4, Red Lion Yard, Old Portsmouth and this is where I entered the world on 17 November 1923 and spent the first nine years of my life. Red Lion Yard was an old coaching house separated from Portsmouth Cathedral by Church Lane and situated between St Thomas' Street and High Street.

There was a pathway from the yard into Church Lane. There was a Smithy run by Mr Baxter on the corner as you came into the yard from St. Thomas' Street. The Red Lion Inn was at the end of the yard on the right. Whymark's grocery shop was in Oyster Street. Butt's Greengrocers and Coal Merchants was in St. Thomas' Street. There was a grocery shop in St. Thomas' Street opposite Red Lion Yard which was owned by a Mr & Mrs Way who were very nice people. The French Onion Store was in Oyster Street and the Onion Johnnies would come on the bicycles to collect the onions to sell around the streets. On Saturdays I can remember having to go to the bakers in Hambrook Street, I don't remember the name but there was a large brewery nearby [Batchelors - Ed]. We always had to get a "Scofa" loaf which was horrible, very hard and brown [a Scottish Soda bread made without yeast - Ed] but we could also get a penny bag of cakes which was a treat.

Flat 4 was tiny with only two rooms and a small wash room on the side. To get from the living room to the one bedroom we had to cross a landing. The whole family slept in one room, all of us children sleeping on one mattress. By the time I was old enough to have any memories, my two oldest brothers Will and John, being much older than me, had left home and joined the Army, but that still left 6 of us living in two rooms.

One of our neighbours was an old lady called Granny Oakes. We children were quite scared of her and called her a witch because she dressed all in black. She was drunk most of the time and she would stand in the yard and yell out to her husband, frightening my sister Kath out of her wits. Another neighbour was called Granny Smith. She had a son, John, and a daughter Dorothy. Mr and Mrs Kerridge lived above us with their sons William (known for some reason as

Church Lane with Red Lion Yard on right

Nonny) and Frederick.

When I was about three years old, the trap door to the cellar of the Red Lion Inn had been left open and I fell in. John Smith came and carried me back up the stairs and poor Nonny Kerridge thought I was dead, he was in quite a state about it but I was only badly bruised.

We were extremely poor and because Dad couldn't work, we were 'living on the Parish' and this had quite a stigma attached to it. The Parish Relief was just 24 shillings a week. A local charity, The Portsmouth Brotherhood, always made sure that we children had clothes and shoes. We always had to wear charity boots as they were sturdy but we hated them. Mum used to housekeep for a very nice lady and her husband and they would give her second hand clothes for us as they had children of similar ages.

One Christmas time I was playing in the yard and a boy came in dragging a Christmas tree, he asked me which flat was No 4 and I said that was where I lived. He then told me the Christmas tree was for us. My brother Will had sent it, I was so excited as I think that this was the first time we had a tree at Christmas. That year Will also sent me a doll, again the first I ever had. I kept that doll for years and still had it when my first daughter was born in 1946. Dad made me a wooden pushchair for the doll and Mum knitted doll's clothes and a blanket for the pushchair. One day after I had been playing in Pembroke Gardens, I got home to find that the blanket was missing. I rushed back to the Gardens and was so relieved to find it hanging on a bush. I played a lot in Pembroke Gardens when I was young and I remember there was a big gun there which we called Big Bertha, we then started to call my sister Big Bertha, although she was anything but big, Dad used to say that if Bertha turned sideways you wouldn't be able to see her. I learned to ride a bike in Pembroke Gardens on a friend's bike.

There was a greengrocer's shop in Pembroke Road, run by a very old lady, where we would get a penny's worth of 'pecked' fruit. This was fruit that had become bruised and was not fit to be sold. Mum would make us jam sandwiches and a bottle of lemonade made up with the lemonade crystals and, with our odd bits of fruit, we would have a picnic in Pembroke Gardens.

We also used to play down by the Camber Docks on the big cable reels jumping from one to the other. One day my sister Bertha and I went to the Camber to play, I don't remember how old I was but Bertha was supposed to be keeping an eye on me. She had other ideas however and went off to play with some boys. They were all throwing stones and one of them landed on Bertha's head. I never told Mum that Bertha had been playing with the boys or she would have been in trouble for not looking after me.

When Will came home for a weekend, he always took me to the Church Parade on Grand Parade before we went to church. I always enjoyed watching the soldiers marching and it made me proud that my big brother was a soldier.

We went to school at Portsmouth Town School in Gunwharf Road. We would walk into St. Thomas' Street, down Lombard Street and into Gunwharf Road. The school was eventually sold to make way for the Electricity Station and then I went to Kent Street School.

The children at Pembroke Gardens

On Sundays we would go the Cathedral, which until 1927 was just St Thomas' Church, for morning service. In the afternoon we children would go to Sunday School at the Cathedral Hall in Pembroke Road and in the evening we would go to the Fisherman's Mission in Warblington Street.

When I was five years old Mum had another baby, my youngest brother Bertie. I was about seven years old when I had to go into the Eye and Ear Hospital in

Pembroke Road to have my tonsils out but instead of taking out my tonsils they took out five of my teeth and in doing so burned my throat. (A definite case for a medical negligence claim these days!) Mum was told that I was to have just bread and milk until my throat was better. When we got home she made me some bread and milk but Bertie made such a fuss that he was given the bread and milk and I had to have some toast, presumably because there was no milk left. My tonsils were eventually taken out when I was about 12.

Just after Bertie's second birthday I was playing in Pembroke Gardens with my friends. It was a Thursday evening. The cathedral bells had been ringing and the big gun that stood in Pembroke Gardens had been fired. When I went home all the neighbours were in the house because Bertie had died. We children didn't go to the funeral but I do remember his little coffin being taken out of the yard. Bertie is buried in Highland Road Cemetery.

About this time my brother Fred was sent away to the Nautical Training School. He was only about 12 years old but he was a bit of a problem to Mum. All he wanted to do was to go on the boats in the Camber and was often brought home by the police when he didn't come home from school. He was not a naughty boy but he had what Mum called wanderlust. There was an old lady called Miss Ida Blackett who lived on Grand Parade and she took a shine to Fred, she always told him that when she died he would get her house, of course it didn't happen. As soon as Fred was old enough he joined the Navy.

When I was nine years old, Red Lion Yard was condemned and eventually demolished and incorporated into the extension to Portsmouth Cathedral. Mum and Dad then rented Flat 5, 110 High Street. This was a very tall house which was divided into six or seven flats. It was a much nicer flat and had two bedrooms, a kitchen and a sitting room. I can't remember what we did for a bathroom. 110 High Street was directly opposite the George Hotel which is where Nelson stayed the night before he left for the Battle of Trafalgar. One day I was playing with my friends Frankie Wilson and Winnie Robb in the cellars of 110 High Street and we found a big black trunk which was full of old fashioned sailors' hats. We also discovered a tunnel so we decided to explore. After we had gone quite a way and were probably halfway across High Street, I got scared because it was very dark and said I didn't want to go any further so we came back.

In 1933 Bertha left school and went to work in North End as a live-in nursery nurse for a family called Glanville who were solicitors. About this time Will married Gwen in Portsmouth Cathedral. Kath and I were bridesmaids and wore green satin dresses edged with fur at the cuffs and collar. We also carried green satin muffs that were edged with fur. This marriage didn't last very long as it turned out that Gwen had forgotten to divorce her first husband so the marriage was bigamous and illegal. I don't know what happened to her but I never saw her again.

In 1935 Will married Mary, again in the Cathedral, and again Kath and I were bridesmaids. This time we wore dresses patterned with sweet peas and carried baskets of flowers. On the morning of the wedding we went to get our hair curled by Mrs Grey in Broad Street but then I had to go school. I had forgotten that it was swimming day so when I came home to get changed for the wedding I had to run down to Broad Sweet and get my hair curled again. I remember wearing this dress again when we went on a day trip to Brighton with the British Legion. Kath left school in 1935 and went to Hawkley Hurst in Dibden, Southampton. This just left me at home.

In 1937 I left school and went to work as a daily help for a lady in Stanley Street but this lasted for only six months because one Thursday when I had taken Mum and Dad to the British Legion meeting in Goldsmith Avenue; she told me that I would have to take Dad home as she was going home on the tram. She was crippled with arthritis by this time and this is the last time I remember her walking. I then had to stay home to look after Mum and Dad.

In 1938 John married Winnie at Freshwater on the Isle of Wight. Bertha was a bridesmaid. In 1939 Fred married Edith in Portsmouth Register Office and they went to live in Cottage Grove and in 1940 they had a son Colin.

My Dad died in February 1939 when I was 16 and he is buried in Milton Cemetery. Shortly after this, when 110 High Street was sold by the landlord, Mum and I moved to a flat at 115 Victoria Road North. The building had steps going up to the front door and we were on the first floor so it was quite an effort coping with Mum and her wheelchair. I remember all the noise and excitement around the area when Pompey won the FA Cup that year and sitting on the gate post to watch the team travelling through the city.

This was where we were living when the Second World War broke out and my sisters Bertha and Kath came back home and joined the NAAFI. Kath was at Eastney Barracks and Bertha was at HMS Nelson and later at Bletchley Park.

Because our flat in Victoria Road North was upstairs, it was not possible for us to stay at 115 Victoria Road North during the war and we moved to a ground floor flat at 40 Campbell Road. Because we would not be able to get Mum out of the house and into an air raid shelter, the cupboard under the stairs was reinforced and a brick wall built just outside the front door. The flat had a sitting room, one bedroom and a kitchen although we had to share a bathroom which was upstairs. Mum slept in the sitting room and we girls shared the bedroom. Bill and Laura Sawyer lived upstairs with their daughter Thelma, who had something wrong with her and died when she was young.

Next door at No 42 lived my old teacher and headmistress, Miss Wade and Miss Phillips and also another lady called Miss Wilkins. One day Miss Wilkins asked me if Mum liked roses so I said yes. A few days later she gave me several rose bushes to plant in the garden. The Revd and Mrs Kinkead lived at No 38 and I remember them telling us they had a son who took part in the Schneider Trophy Race. When we moved into the flat, I planted lots of wild flower seeds in the front garden which all came up and looked beautiful, all the neighbours commented on them. In the back garden there was an apple tree and a pear tree and throughout the war I grew vegetables.

In 1941 an unexploded bomb landed two doors away from 40 Campbell Road and we had to be evacuated while it was dealt with. We went to stay with Mum's friend Mrs Knight in Montgomery Road as she was the only one whose house could accommodate Mum's wheelchair. We had packed a box of food to take with us which included a joint of pork, however when we got to Mrs Knight's we discovered that we had forgotten the pork but we were not allowed to go back and get it. We were, in fact, not allowed back home for three weeks so when we did eventually get home, the joint of pork almost walked out to meet us! It was horrible and such a terrible waste of food in those days of rationing. On the day that the bomb was eventually moved, all the streets in the area were evacuated. I believe the bomb was taken to Eastney and exploded. This is when I met my first husband, Charlie, as Mrs Knight was his grandmother.

Early in 1942 with the fall of Singapore we got the news from John's wife Winnie that he had been taken prisoner by the Japanese. In September that year we heard that he had died. He was given a full military funeral and is buried in Kranji Cemetery in Singapore. With the war and Fred being away in the Navy, Edith had difficulty in coping and at the end of 1943 Fred came round to Campbell Road with Colin and told us that he and Edith had separated and he wanted Mum and me to have custody of Colin while he was away so we went to Court and got custody and Edith had access on Saturdays.

In 1943 Kath married Gordon in St Mary's Church. I was her Maid of Honour and Fred gave her away. They went to live in Cottage View which was off of Arundel Street. I made the wedding cake and did the catering for her reception which was held at Campbell Road. In 1944 I married Charlie and again I made the cake and did the catering. Our reception was held at Campbell Road. Bertha was my Maid of Honour and Will gave me away. In the summer of 1945 we were invited to the wedding of the Reverend Jock Fletcher- Campbell who was a family friend and we were all getting ready when Fred came round and told us to pack Colin's things as he and Edith were getting back together. As we were walking to the Cathedral for the wedding, a car passed by and Colin was in the back, he waved to us and that was the last time I saw him. In December 1945 Bertha married Ted and although I didn't make the cake this time, I did do the catering for the reception which was again held at Campbell Road. I was the Matron of Honour and Will gave her away.

In September 1946 I gave birth to my first daughter in 40 Campbell Road. During this time with so many of us living in the flat, Bertha and Ted slept in a house across the road and came back to No 40 during the day. Fred and Edith had moved to St. Thomas' Street and one evening in November 1946, whilst Fred was again away in the Navy, Edith had boiled up the water in the tin bath for Colin and put it on the floor. Colin had taken off his clothes ready for his bath and just had his shoes and socks on and before Edith had time to add the cold water Colin fell in. He was taken to hospital and Edith came round to get Mum to take her to the hospital. Fred was rushed home by the Navy but he didn't make it before Colin died of his injuries. Colin is buried in Milton Cemetery.

After the war 40 Campbell Road was to be sold so Charlie and I applied to the Council for one of the houses on the newly built Council Estate at Paulsgrove, because Mum and Bertha and Ted were also living at Campbell Road they agreed to let us have a house if we all went together. We moved to 119 Allaway Avenue in January 1947 during the worst weather experienced in a long time. Snow and ice covered the ground for weeks and we had no idea what the garden of the house looked like until the spring when the snow eventually melted. Because of the weather conditions we were unable to dig up Mum's rose bushes to bring with us but years later whenever we passed 40 Campbell Road we would see Mum's rose bushes still there. Mr Bath our coalman did the removal for us. Bertha stayed with Mum and came up with Mr Bath and Kath and I went up to the house on the bus to get a fire going before Mum got there. Unfortunately my marriage to Charlie ended in divorce in 1947 and in 1948 I met my second husband Bill.

119 Allaway Avenue had an L shaped living room and Mum, being unable to get up the stairs, had her bed in the front half of the room. On the evening of 10

December 1949 I was sitting in front of the fire with Bertha and I just couldn't get warm. At about 10 o'clock I went over to see Mum and found her dead. She was buried with Dad in Milton Cemetery.

In February 1950 Bill and I left Paulsgrove and went to find somewhere to live back in Portsmouth. We moved around for a while renting rooms wherever we could, including Shearer Road and Beecham Road and eventually renting a caravan in Milton Road.

By this time I was expecting my second daughter and Bill's Mum and Dad said that No 2 Stamford Street in Fratton had come up for sale and that they would given us the deposit for it if we all moved in together. So in 1950 we moved in and all lived together until Bill's Mum died in 1952 shortly before my third daughter was born. Bill and I had four daughters altogether and my eldest daughter thought of him as her Dad too, eventually changing her name to his. No 2 Stamford Street was a terraced house opening straight onto the Street. There were three bedrooms and three reception rooms with a scullery. The lavatory was outside and there was no bathroom. We had to bring the old tin bath into the

The rear of 2 Stamford Street

kitchen on bath nights. Bill's Mum and Dad had the middle room downstairs as their bedroom. After Bill's Dad died in 1960, we had a bath fitted in the scullery. Stamford Street ran from St John's Road to Fratton Road and No 2 was the first house on the right coming in from St John's Road. When we moved in our next door neighbour at No 4 was Mrs Anscombe but she eventually moved to Liverpool. Clifton Street and Wimpole Street both crossed over Stamford Street on the way down to Fratton Road.

There were a couple of little shops and the Bethel Mission, where we used to go to church, in St. John's Road and this is where one of my daughters met her husband. My three older girls went to Besant Road School and the younger two went to Arundel Street School.

When I met Bill he was working on the buses but he then went to work for the Dockyard in the Royal Naval Base. We didn't have a car and as was common with all the 'Dockies' at that time Bill used to cycle to work. Our family outings in the summer months were mostly spent on the seafront. We would walk down to the common and have a picnic and the children would play in the paddling pool. There was also a little train that ran along the seafront.

If the weather was fine on Sunday's after church, we would all go for a long walk, sometimes down Victoria Road North to the seafront and other times along Fratton Road. At the beginning of 1964, Bill was not feeling well so he went to see the doctor who told him it was gastroenteritis and signed him off sick for a week. He had another appointment for the next week but on 24 January Bill died of bowel cancer. He was 58 years old. Bill is buried in Milton Cemetery.

I was 41 years old with five children to bring up, my youngest daughter was only five. Times were tough but we were a happy family. Just after Bill died, 2 Stamford Street was compulsorily purchased by the Council and I was allocated a house at Leigh Park and this was the end of my memories of living in Portsmouth."

Peggy Gast

The final memories deal with childhood in Paulsgrove

Paulsgrove

The First Five Years

"I am unsure of when we moved from Yorkshire to Portsmouth, and to what address but dad was sent to the dockyard as a marine coppersmith. I remember nothing of my first two years, but mother told me much later that I had asked her not to let the 'Jerrys' get me. This referred to the German bombing of Portsmouth which forced families into air-raid shelters. Some of these shelters were to be used as garden sheds long after the war ended.

Nomadic as we were, our next move, when I was two in 1943, was to Dunstaffnage, near Oban in Scotland. I do slightly remember my next two years, but the reason for going there and description of it was thankfully recently given to me by our next door neighbours there, based on reminiscing newspaper cuttings.

The village, built on the foundations of the old Dunstaffnage military camp, was created to house the Admiralty Dockyard workers who were ordered north to work on ship repairs in the relative safety of a West Highlands bay, well away from the heavy bombing inflicted on southern England. The buildings, comprising Nissen huts and prefabricated houses, were put up virtually overnight by Royal Marine engineers. A floating dock, plus a workshop built in the grounds of Dunstaffnage Castle, were used by workers for repairing ships damaged in the North Atlantic. Prefabs were in pairs, i.e. semidetached, and we were in No 17B, with no road name. Alongside was No 17A, with Fred Brown, again from Portsmouth dockyard, with his wife Rose, and daughter Joan, then nine years old. There was also a younger son, of whom I know nothing.

I understand that, because this was a new community with workers and their families from the south of England, social events were brought into play, with dancing, pantomimes and even a weekly film show, becoming an English village in the heart of the West Highlands. However, because the local Laird felt his estate at Dunstaffnage was somehow devalued by having council houses within its boundaries, he later pulled strings and had the name changed to Dunbeg. My brother, Anthony Stuart Lindsay, was born on Saturday 26th February 1944, but I recall nothing about him or anyone else all the time I was there. My only memory was in running from the prefab down a field with a friend to the country road and seeing a car. This friend, whose name escapes me was to remain so when we returned to Portsmouth.

At or before the end of the war in 1945 our neighbours, the Browns, moved back to Portsmouth to live in 84 Agincourt Road as rent-payers. Many years later they were to buy it. Soon after this, we moved to be with them in the same rather crowded house, and presumably paid our share of the rent. In January 1946, one month before my 5th birthday, I started at Wellington Place school, just around the corner from home.

My academic prowess was lessened on more than one occasion, by being sent home, on my own, for my habit of wetting myself in school. This was probably by my reluctance to put up my hand for permission to go to the loo so often, but, fifty or more years on, I was to learn that I had a bladder problem which was resolved after a simple operation.

I remember just two more things whilst I lived there. The first was mother constantly putting off buying me sweets, as I was reminded that I nagged her by saying 'sweeties in the next shop mummy?' The next shop never existed! The other memory was of me collecting, for some obscure reason, matchsticks in the so called garden and the seven year older Joan saying "boo". I Think that, if I had known bad language at that age, I would have used it, but I had an understandable aversion to girls for some while after. Ironically, after we moved from there in 1947, I had no contact with them until many years later, when I responded to the newspaper article on Dunstaffnage and Joan and I re-met in 2010, her mother Rose died at the age of 94, Fred having passed away years before.

Paulsgrove and Wymering

I have always had a love for Portsmouth, having lived there or in its surrounds for most of my life. Between the age of six and 18 I lived in the districts of Paulsgrove and Wymering and so, before I go further, I should like to explain some of the geography of those places.

The original and main part of Portsmouth is an island separated from the mainland to its north by the narrow Port Creek, and called Portsea Island - hence the Southern area by Portsmouth Harbour called Portsea, where my mother was born. The island was originally connected to the mainland only by east and west bridges and a railway line. The west one was called Portsbridge, and the road over it went 70 miles onto London. To the east of this road is Cosham and to the west is Wymering, and their, and thus Portsmouth's northern border is Portsdown Hill.

The large area of Paulsgrove continues west of Wymering to meet up with Portsmouth's western border at Portchester. In the 1930's the first houses were built in Wymering, mainly on what was referred to as the 'Isle of Wight' estate since the roads were named after places there. In the south east of Paulsgrove, in and off Cheltenham Road houses were also built in that period. In each case, the reason seems to be because of the slum clearance of Portsea. Building up the rest of Wymering, and most of Paulsgrove, started to take place after the 2nd World

War, due to the intensive bombing there. So I will now move up to Paulsgrove.

Aged 6 to 10
I have plenty of memories from the age of six, but don't necessarily remember or know all the dates. I will do my best, though it is improbable that I will be criticized where I am wrong, due to the limited number of innocent readers. I have recently seen my National Insurance Identity Card dated 30th June 1947, with 17 Abbeydore Road, Paulsgrove, Portsmouth as the address, and it is probable that we moved to there in May of that year. It is unlikely that my family had furniture to move from Agincourt Road, though I may be wrong, but I clearly remember walking to Kingston Crescent (together with our black cat Mickey) to catch the Corporation red double-decker 'B' bus to Allaway Avenue, the nearest stop to Abbeydore Road.

17 Abbeydore Road

The houses, two floored terraced, were provided by the Canadians and assembled by ex Italian prisoners-of-war and, though considered temporary, exist all over Paulsgrove to this day. Unlike our previous homes, we had three bedrooms, a bathroom and toilet and linen cupboard upstairs, and an L-shaped living room and kitchen downstairs, in addition to a long garden. In a conservatory attached to the kitchen there were coal and coke bunkers to feed the living room fire and the kitchen boiler used to wash clothes. I am unsure of how the bath and other water was heated, but I do remember that due to cost, or perhaps habit, baths were taken only once a week, usually on a Sunday, before school or work the following day. For the same reason, clothes were normally only washed weekly, though changed more frequently. Sunday dinner was always roast beef, the cheapest meat, and chicken was a rarity only for Christmas. Bones from the beef were used to provide Monday's stew.

Shortly after moving in, three lots of four terraced houses were brick-built in the conventional way, in spaces between the prefabricated ones. I remember being sent across to them with cups of tea for the workers, in exchange for firewood from the window frames - a fair exchange.

The main shopping centre was about half a mile away in Allaway Avenue, as a block of ten corrugated iron Nissen huts with a common front, of which the Co-op had three or four units. The name Co-op derives from Portsea Island Mutual Cooperative Society Ltd., or PIMCO, and it gave a yearly dividend to its customers. Double seven, five three two - 77532 stays in my mind as the number given to the cashier each time we bought something. Most food and other goods were rationed during the war and for years after, and the ration book had to be presented. Things now taken for granted such as plastic wrapping for food were not available; butter and margarine etc., were cut to size and put in paper; sugar was weighed and put into blue paper bags. Bread was uncovered, even when, as requested, a loaf was cut in half. We did not complain, because we had known no difference and the Health and Safety Act had not yet come into play. Hillside School, now called Paulsgrove Primary School, was completed in about 1950, but the original buildings, when I went in 1947, consisted of one long white hut, opposite three black ones. Between 1948 and 1950 the school increased size greatly. The infants' and I think first two years of juniors' classes were mixed, and the third and fourth years were separated sexes. In one of the classes I sat next to Sandra Bumstead from Allaway Avenue. I am sure she has changed her name. In another, David Higgs, who has the same birth date as me, occupied the window seat next to me, I have recently made contact with him to recharge my memory. I only remember two others. One, whose name I don't recall, drowned over the weekend, and everyone knew about it but the teacher. The other one was the younger brother of 'Ginger' Russell, who died from leukemia, an illness whose name was to haunt me over sixty years later.

During the building of the new school, for a year or so I was transferred to Wymering Primary School in Southampton Road, now called Medina Primary

School in Medina Road - same school and road but changed names. It was very interesting recently to visit both schools, though no-one seemed to remember me - I don't know why! Discipline was strict, and the slap, plimsoll and cane were frequently used on 'guilty' pupils, though it never happened to the goodie me. I do recall, when I was about eight, witnessing a girl having her knickers removed for a spanking by the lady teacher for bad writing. My innocent thoughts at that time were solely the hope it did not happen to me: I cannot imagine what penalty the teacher would receive if it were to happen now. Discipline out of the classroom was assured by prefects, who reported mis-doings to the teacher, and, for lunchtimes, dinner monitors (of which I was one) were appointed.

At the end of each play period the head teacher would blow a whistle, at which point all would have to freeze, even if they had not been moving. On the second whistle the pupils would run to form a class group then march to the classroom. In class, if a pupil needed to use the toilet, the blackboard duster would have to be collected so that its absence would indicate the toilet was already in use, and thus avoid meetings away from class.

My final year at Hillside School started in September 1951 in class 4A. The teacher was Mr Street, and his dress and character were recalled to me with a letter from a friend, Roger Russell, who lived three doors away from me in Paulsgrove. Mr Street had no car, so travelled by Southdown bus from Horndean or Clanfield. He dressed, summer and winter, in a thick tweed suit just like a farmer, plus a pork pie hat with a green feather in the brim. In 1952 I sat and passed my 11 plus exam.

In about 1949 I joined the 63rd Portsmouth Cubs, which took place at St Michael & All Angels Church. At that time the church was a prefabricated concrete hut. It was divided, at about two thirds of its length, into a large area which was the church hall where cubs, scouts and other bodies like the Mothers' Union met, and the other third, behind large green folding doors held the Altar and Vestry etc. The vicar was Father Kilvert, and his wife was the Akela in charge of the cubs. I was in the 'Red Six and remember my badge earners included tests in ironing clothes and even using the public telephone. It was rare for people to have telephones in the house, hence the need to use this device in an emergency. The call I made meant I put four pennies into the slot, dialled the number and, when answered, pressed button 'A'. The message was "Mr Brown has been knocked down by a Southdown bus. He is now in hospital but is recovering". If the message had not been received, money was recovered by pressing button 'B'. About sixty years later, the local paper referred to St

St Michael & All Angels Cubs

Michael's celebrating its 50th Anniversary which, in my tired brain could not be so, until I realised it was the 'new' church which took the place of the one I knew. On the way from home to the cubs I passed a house which had an H shaped TV aerial on a long flag pole in the garden - another rare sighting in those days.

I am unsure of why I had an interest in playing the piano, but I used to walk to the middle of Paulsgrove once a week for lessons with a Mrs Birch. I must have been promising because my parents bought an upright piano for the house, at which I practised nightly, much to the dis-amusement of my dad, whose radio (then called wireless) was being interrupted. My mother worked at the laundry in Portsmouth some evenings and my dad took advantage at these times by disallowing me more than a token practise. In May 1953 I passed my Trinity College of Music Initial Division with Honours, but then ceased lessons, thereafter playing 'by ear'.

I am sure that, in this day and age, children in possession of mobile phones, computers and other electronic devices, still congregate in groups and play games. However, in my time, the latter was the only answer to fulfilling our needs. Boys and girls formed their own groups or gangs with a leader, and seldom mixed except for games like hopscotch, where physical ability was not in question. Girls would, much to my dis-amusement, do handstands against a wall, showing their navy blue knickers. Boys played 'hit', marbles (or alleys) and hide and seek, most of this taking place on the road without the threat of traffic. No-one in our road possessed a car, and the only motorized transport was the dustbin lorry, bread van, milk 'float' and ice-cream van.

Rain never stopped play except where chalk marks on the pavements and road were washed away. At one end of our road was a field we called 'the humps and bumps' which was an area where waste earth and stones from building the houses were deposited, making high mounds where we played endlessly. When it was necessary to play indoors I went to see Roger Russell at No 11, who had a model electric railway which was so much better than my unrealistic clockwork one which my dad had bought years before and added to each Christmas. Roger's father lost a leg towards the end of the war and I remember being either frightened or mesmerized by a wooden replacement in a cupboard - I should have been less nosy! Christmas was fun. Tony and I were put to bed on the eve, and were kept informed of Santa Claus' whereabouts with updates every five minutes - even before the days of 'sat-com', On his arrival, he came upstairs to see us, and looking like a very old man in all his splendour including his large white beard. He asked what we wanted and said that we would then need to sleep until the morning. Early on Christmas Day we would notice stockings (literally) on the bed ends containing temporary gifts and an apple, to keep us going until the main presents were given downstairs. Before we came downstairs we had to wait at the top and hear the wireless playing 'God save the King'. The presents had been laid unwrapped in separate piles on the floor by Santa Claus, and we frantically delved into it all, without noticing our parents and aunt Kath opening theirs. Decorations in the house at Christmas were plentiful but all hand made. We were unaware of the fact that Santa Claus was our dad until, when I was about eight, aunt Kath looked after us while mother and dad were on holiday in Scotland. Tony found the Father Christmas outfit in a kitchen cupboard and told Kath about it, but, instead of saying it had been left there to be washed, she 'confessed' to him not existing and saying it had been dad all the time. It was an inappropriate revelation to eight and five year olds, but aunt Kath was ever a very lovely person in all her other ways.

There were only two other incidents in Abbeydore Road I would refer to, the first one being the 'Bobby Sadler action'. He lived in the brick house No 27 and was at the losing end of a battle with me one day. His mother came out to slap my face and, on receipt of this information, my mother went to No 27 and slapped her face and advised her not to repeat her misdemeanor. At No 29 was a girl called Ann Ferris, who, obviously a few years older than me, won the Miss Southsea Contest - some claim to fame for the road.

Our brother Richard Brian was born on 14th September 1950, but was never a well baby. I remember the doctor visiting and, although I had never changed a nappy, was told to 'clear up the mess' Richard had made. I was not best pleased with this order, because nappies were not disposable then, but cleaned by boiling water after dispensing with the 'solid bits' down the loo. Sadly, Richard died at the age of ten months on 20th July 1951. This was to be the reason for us shortly moving to a prefab in Wymering.

Clacton Road

I am unsure of when we moved to 31 Clacton Road, Wymering, but it was not before February 6th 1952. On this date King George VI died and I remember as the result being sent home from school to Abbeydore Road in respect, and saying in my innocence, 'guess who's died, we've got the day off'. My long term loyalty as a Royalist did not exist at that time when not quite 11 years old.

The single floor white prefab was compact but adequate, with three bedrooms, including one for aunt Kath, who was still with us. The kitchen was also the dining room and laundry and later would become the area for dad scratch building his model ship HMS Solebay. Many years later I was to emulate his works by building the same ship as a working model, and the interest continues to this day. The living room had all the chairs facing the open coal fire, as television did not overtake our lives until years later. Instead we listened to the wireless, via the Radio Rentals device, with so much interest each evening. Football and boxing matches had good commentaries and though I was uninterested in either they were easy to follow. However, programmes like 'Journey into Space' - a tale of the future - occupied my otherwise vacant brain by trying to visualize travelling to Mars in half an hour, long before space travel became a reality.

Working days in the dockyard were from 7 a.m. to 5 p.m., and dad always rode his bike the several miles, he never used a car. The many hours overtime, including weekends, meant that I rarely saw him other than in the evenings until my bedtime, which was strictly timed. Tony, being three years younger, saw even less of him, but the time we had with him is still precious in our memories. A dual carriage road [Southampton Road - Ed] now from Cosham to the M27 was at that time a long narrow field in which we played, as it was just a few yards from the block of prefabs. Clacton Road was busy with traffic and not as appropriate as Abbeydore for marbles and hopscotch. My friends were all new, and more so when I joined Portsmouth Building School (PBS) in September1952. The idea of this school was to encourage pupils to take up building trades, following these needs after the war. Those who took up such trades had the usual five-year apprenticeship reduced by one year. However, the school had the same high academic standards as the Grammar and Technical schools, so no-one escaped this until they left at the age of sixteen. PBS was situated in a number of different locations, but the first two years were at Cosham Park House in Cosham Park Avenue, now a Doctors' surgery. Assemblies each morning were at Cosham Civic Centre, and a number of hutments off Cosham High Street were used for technical drawing, and plumbing. Painting & decorating and bricklaying were taught miles away in Greetham Street, near Portsmouth Guildhall. In the third to fifth years the building used was Portsea Parish Institute in Fratton Road. This later became the site for Radio Victory, and is now a block of flats. Alongside this school was the Vicarage for St Mary's Church. In the grounds at the back, the school practised the sports of discus and javelin throwing. This was under the doubtful jurisdiction of the disliked Welsh Sports Master. Because of the limited number of javelins, pupils formed two lines parallel to their paths of travel, to collect them when they landed, so that they didn't miss their turns. Unfortunately for me the one I was to collect bounced off the ground into my right lower leg. I didn't use the 'gosh' word in those days but was not best pleased. Although I did expect sympathy, understanding and medical help, the Sports' Master called me a 'stupid boy' several times. In this day and age he would have been dismissed, if employed at all. No ambulance was called, but instead dad was sent from the dockyard and arrived on his bike. He waited with me for the normal bus service and rode to meet me at the hospital. There was no rebound on this accident, and when I returned to school it was as if nothing had happened - certainly no financial compensation as would be the case nowadays. Our sister Linda was born in St Mary's Hospital on Tuesday 22 June 1954. Sadly, she was not to live a long life and started it with being taken to Great Ormond Street Hospital for Children in London 70 miles away, before she was a day old. This was to remove a blockage in her stomach and thankfully she overcame this. It was later found that she had Fibrosystic Disease of the Pancreas, from which she died nearly five years later. The Pancreas is part of the digestive system, and in order to make it work properly it was necessary to take Pancreatin before each meal. This was a very fine powder mixed with water in a thick cream form. Pancreatin was from the Pancreas of specially bred pigs not a pretty thought, but it worked, and there was no shame in it. At about this time Kath moved out of the prefab because of the accommodation change, and lived in Kingston, Portsmouth. At the same time she opened a dressmaker shop in Chichester Road called Cherry's, and mother worked part time with her. When I was in my third year in PBS, dad and I went to Kath's house at lunch time, while she was at work, and re-heated food she'd prepared for us. The note left usually said 'din and pud in oven - heat on gas No 7 for 20 minutes'. There was no refrigerator in the house but we still survived. Dad's Triumph car was kept spotlessly clean but rarely used, and parked in nearby Wivenhoe Close. Few people had cars in those days, so it was on its own with the Somerset registration YD 9152. A regular habit was to make me take the battery to a garage in Cosham for it to be charged for 24 hours because, although the engine was started using a crank handle, its usage was too low for the dynamo to carry out this task.

When I was 14 I started a paper delivery round for Dodd & Reed in Cosham. This was delivery of about 60 newspapers mornings and evenings 6 days a week, and just the morning on Sundays. Christmas day in 1955 was a Sunday and deliveries were made on that day with no exceptions. The 13 rounds earned 10 shillings (50p) a week which was four times the pocket money I had received until then. I say this, because I no longer received this and also had to give mother half of my 10 shillings. This meant that she received three times the amount she used to pay me, and I did 13 rounds for just double my pocket money. I added to this by doing extra rounds if paper boys were unwell, and also a money collection round on Saturdays. Mother also collected half of this extra so I learned to 'pay my way'. Of course dad was the real culprit behind mother, but I thought he had changed his financial outlook when he arrived home by bike 'towing' another new one. The bike was for me and I showed my endless gratitude until I realised I had to pay for it weekly as he had only paid the deposit. Again, the 'gosh' word was spoken under my breath. For some obscure reason, our address changed from 31 Clacton Road to 7 Wivenhoe Close, though it was the same house. I think it was in 1956 that we moved to Herne Road.

Herne Road

Across the long narrow field was, and still is, Herne Road, between 6th Avenue and Wymering Lane. The three floored L shaped block of flats was not named, and we were at No 12 on the ground floor. It was like the prefab but bigger and more comfortable and had a balcony, to enjoy the sun in the south. The dual carriage road was constructed while we were there. From the age of 16 my social circle expanded, which coincided with the introduction of 'Rock and Roll' music and the wearing of 'Teddy Boy' clothes. In the early 1900s, when King Edward 7th (hence Teddy) was on the Throne, long un-waisted (or 'drape') black coats were worn, together with narrow legged trousers and high collared white shirts. This, together with the hair style, became a long term fashion in the 1950s for teenaged boys.

In the summer of 1957, when I left school, I took the Dockyard entrance exam and went to Scotland on holiday, but was called back early by dad when the results were known. I had come 8th in Britain and 6th in Portsmouth, so had the choice of trades and started my 5-year apprenticeship as an Electrical Fitter in September. One day and two evenings a week were spent at the Dockyard College, with the intention of qualifying at the end of five years for entry to Durham University for a Degree in the subject. Although I was academically sound, my social events and laziness resulted in my leaving the College after two years, with no 'bits of paper, though years later I would make up for it.

In the first two years the practical learning was in hutments in Conway Street, just outside the Dockyard's Unicorn Gate. For the first nine months of this time 'Navy test jobs' were boringly imposed on us, teaching the use of tools, particularly files, and accuracy to within one thousandth of an inch. In the remaining time before moving into the Dockyard there were more practical and interesting elements of electrical engineering, almost as a reward after the filing. The downside was the punishment for wrong doings - in my case the handing of cigarettes to schoolgirls passing by. The sentence for this and other misdemeanors was to be sent back to the filing section and carry out more Navy test jobs.

In the evenings and weekends boys (blokes or mushters) and girls (sorts), in separate groups, walked in Cosham High Street or met in pubs, mostly the 'George and Dragon' (though of course with no alcohol) and gradually paired up. This also happened at Hillside Youth Club on Friday nights, where a local band played rock and roll to which we 'bopped', which just about passed for dancing. My apprentice's wages were very low, compared with my friends' who were so well paid as building labourers. However, I later realised that this situation reversed and in the meantime I managed. In the first year my weekly earnings of £2-12s were halved when mother got £1-6s, or 26 shillings *(26/-)*. The cost of buying a £6-6s suit was 6/- per week for 21 weeks and this was paid for each Saturday at North End, some miles away. Haircuts, visiting cinemas (flicks), 10 cigarettes, and a pint of beer were each one shilling and sixpence *(1/6d* or seven and a half pence in new money). Contraceptives, in the form of a 'packet of 3' were bought for 3/9d at the barbers each Saturday ('something for the weekend

Sir?').

At 17 I took driving lessons with Hampshire Driving Academy, my tutor being Robert Slack. Driving was obviously much easier then but I still felt good about passing my test. As the result I went to Scotland with my friends Colin Baker (who was 19 and owned the car), Sid Smith, and my brother Tony. The 524 miles to Dundee took about 20 hours due to the absence of motorways and by-passes, although the AA route map showed the way as easily as would today's Sat Nav. We travelled to Aberdeen, Glasgow, and camped at Loch Ness but saw no monster there. Coming back home was downhill so only took 18 hours!

In that year Linda was taught embroidery by mother and Kath, and became so good at it that, just before her 4th Birthday, she appeared in the local paper. This was the Evening News of June 4th 1958 and gave a good write up about her abilities, with a photograph of her and dad's model of HMS Solebay in the background. Years later I appeared in the same newspaper with my model of the ship, but my pride of Linda's abilities far outweighed, and still does, that for myself.

On the third floor of our flats were the McKilroys, including the girls Helen, a year younger than me, and Ann, younger still. Although I was in bed by 11 at night I was mentally forced to be envious when looking out of the window on Fridays to see her return from dancing, with her apparently rich boyfriend, in a sports car. I think this is why I started properly dating Diana Legg, who lived with her parents and brother in a block of flats in Cosham. It would be inappropriate for me to detail my times there, but we were to get married when I finished my apprenticeship. Linda was unwell in hospital, and when I came home late on April 29th 1959 the McIlroys were also there and I wondered why. I said to mother 'how's Lindy Loo'? She had died that evening and my world fell apart. Later that year we move to Meonstoke House in Portsmouth."

Robert Lindsay

.

The following list details the books we have produced over the years in chronological order. Titles in bold are still in print.

New Road Trail	1980
Memories of Lake Road	1980
Memories of Childhood	1980
Memories of Church St School	1980
Saturday/Sunday	1980
Memories of Arundel Street	1980
Going to Work	1981
Going to Work II	1981
Pompey Boy	1981
Point Boy	1981
Sixty Two Years a Fratton Pharmacist	1981
Memories of Downtown Portsmouth	1981
Old Southsea Trails	1981
Gateway to Queen Street	1982
Portsmouth at War	1983
Memories of Kingston Road	1983
Portsmouth at War Vol 2	1984
Memories of a Window Dresser	1985
Memories of St Agathas School	1985
Memories of Albert Road	1985
Memories of Charlotte Street	1987
Memories of Fawcett Road	1988
New Road Trail, Revised	1988
Going to Work 3	1988
Going to Work 4	1988
Bygone Days	1988
Memories of Kingston, Revised	1989
Portsea	1989
Memories of Elm Grove & Kings Road	1989
Memories of Stamshaw	1990
Portsmouth's War Time Women	1990
Childhood Memories	1990
Memories of Arundel Street, Revised	1990
Memories of Albert Road	1990
Gateway to Queen Street, Revised	1990
The Quest for Knowledge	1991
Memories of Old Buckland	1991
Old Portsmouth & Spice Island	1992
Memories of Charlotte Street, Revised	**1993**
Shipwright Apprentice	1993

Somerstown as it Was	1993
Memories of Eastney	**1994**
Memories of Downtown, Revised	**1994**
Memories of Over the Lines	1995
Milton Memories	**1996**
Memories of Fratton	**1997**
Memories of Wymering & Paulsgrove	**1998**
Kingston Road Remembered	**1998**
Memories of Marylebone	**1999**
Memories of Lake Road, Revised	1999
Memories of Southsea	**2000**
Memories of Old Buckland, Revised	**2001**
Going to Work Vol. 1, Revised	**2001**
Going to Work Vol. 2, Revised	**2002**
Highbury Memories	**2002**
Memories of Arundel Street, Revised	**2002**
Memories of Mile End	**2004**
Memories of North End & Hilsea	**2006**
Memories of Portsea	**2007**
Memories of Old Portsmouth	**2010**
Memories of Copnor	**2011**
Memories of New Road	**2012**
Dickensian Portsmouth	**2012**

This booklet was compiled by the members of the W.E.A. Local History Group which meets at the Buckland Community Centre, Malins Road, Buckland. The group is made up of local people who wish to record the history of ordinary peoples' lives and the streets in which they live. The group is very informal and welcomes new members who care to come to Malins Road on a Tuesday evening or write to us.

Class Members:
Christine Bessant, Ken Brown, Anton Cox (Secretary), Alan Eamey, Peter Galvin (Chairman), Shirley Jones, Robin Kay, Helen Kryemadhi, Stephen Pomeroy (Editor), Sue Simmonds, Don Tallack, Ron Thompson, Sylvia Webb, Margaret Webster (Treasurer)

Contributors:
Mrs Eddings, Kenneth Frampton, Peggy Gast, Robert Lindsey

References:
Portsmouth City Council Planning Department, Library & Museum and Record Service; The News.

Photographs of Kingston House (DA/2/B/694/2), Kingston Crescent (DA/2/B/694/3) and Regent Cinema (169A/1/4) reproduced by permission of Portsmouth Museum and Records Service with whom the copyright remains.
Photographs of Paulsgrove, Pembroke Gardens and Stamford Street courtesy of the contributors, other photographs from the collection of Stephen Pomeroy.

First published in 2013.

WEA (Portsmouth Branch Local History Group)
Buckland Community Centre
Malins Road
Buckland
Portsmouth

ISBN 978 1 873911 30 3

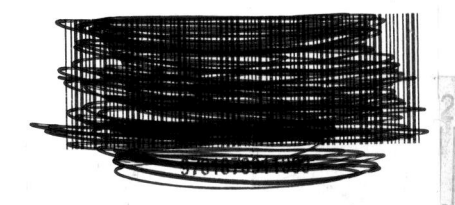

Typeset & Printed in England
by
Printcraft, 108 Marmion Road, Southsea, Hants.